# DORSET
## BEFORE THE CAMERA

1. *(Overleaf)* Lyme Regis in 1796.

DAVID BURNETT

# DORSET
## BEFORE THE CAMERA

### 1539-1855

DOVECOTE PRESS

Text © David Burnett 1982

*First published in 1982 by The Dovecote Press
Stanbridge, Wimborne, Dorset*

ISBN 0 9503518 7 3

Printed by Biddles Ltd
Guildford, Surrey

# Contents

Towns                     *illustration numbers*    2 -  17

Markets & Trade                                    18 -  36

Royal Seaside                                      37 -  43

Castles & Churches                                 44 -  58

People                                             59 -  69

Shipwrecks                                         70 -  78

Pastimes & Pleasures                               79 -  89

Country Life                                       90 -  99

Ports & Harbour                                   100 - 125

Transport                                         126 - 134

# Introduction

To the people of Dorset, the year 1539 seemed certain to be uneventful. Henry VIII was king, and poised between marriages. But the monarch's marital problems had never made much impact on his subjects in the shires, and could safely be ignored. More importantly, the winter had been mild, and, as it drew to a close, lines of pack-horses began moving along the drove roads that linked Dorset to London, their panniers brimming with wine, salt, cloth and fish. Beneath market crosses scattered the length of the county pedlars started touting their wares. Ships ventured to sea, oxen were hitched to the plough. Wagons clattered into cloth towns laden with raw wool for the narrow coarse-woven cloths like 'kersey' and 'Dorset dozens' that were the county's main contribution to the national exchequer. The seasons' wheel had begun turning, and only the foolhardy or farsighted would have dared predict that the year ahead was to mark a watershed in Dorset's history. And then, in early March, the two royal commissioners responsible for the dissolution of the monasteries crossed the county border. In the fortnight that followed, virtually all the monastic houses in Dorset fell victim to the Reformation. Milton Abbey was the first to fall, Shaftesbury the last. It was as absolute as it must have been bewildering. By the end of the month, a way of life that had endured since before the Norman Conquest was finally over. Buildings were surrendered to the crown, then sold — only to be stripped of their stone, timbers and roof lead. The monastic estates became the king's property. Overnight, entire parishes exchanged a spiritual for a secular landlord. Like a stone dropped in water, the ripples caused by the dissolution spread outward into every cottage in the county, dominating gossip and leaving uncertainty in their wake. To many it must have seemed that the only world they knew had been shaken and turned inside out.

Against such a background, a commission was appointed to survey the Dorset coast and suggest how best it could be defended against the threat of invasion by the French. By April a list of recommendations had been put to the Council. The practical outcome of the commission's findings was a small fort on Brownsea Island and castles at Sandsfoot and Portland, to safeguard Portland Roads. Sadly, the fort proposed for Poole was never built, and although Portland Castle still stands, the sole remaining relic from that survey is a map of the Dorset coast. The map itself is nearly four feet long and two feet high. Age and neglect have done little to improve its condition, but it is both the earliest

surviving map to cover most of Dorset and the section showing Lyme Regis provides the opening date for this book (illustration no. 120).

The links between a map and the changes inspired by the dissolution are of course no more than coincidence. Yet curiously, the anonymous cartographer who drew the map of 1539 succeeded in evoking Dorset's character at a time when one way of life was drawing to a close and another was about to begin. No matter that the scale is all wrong, oaks are in leaf in hand-painted woods and the houses have both windows and doors. Errors are common, but the ships huddled in the lee of the Cobb suggest the harbour's attractions more effectively than many a more modern map. Yet already there is a contradiction. If it is the inaccuracies in an illustration that provide its appeal, is that illustration to be trusted? Here we come face to face with the single most relevant difference between the photograph and engraving or drawing. The camera records exactly what it sees, yet there are probably only a handful of illustrations in the whole of this book that scrupulously document what the artist saw. But that should spoil no one's pleasure, nor should it be allowed to detract from their value as a visual history of the strands that make up Dorset's past. Ultimately, both lens and pencil share a similar defect: neither can do more than provide glimpses and impressions of the world they attempt to depict.

By the end of the 16th century a new and more recognizable Dorset was gradually beginning to emerge. The age of Elizabeth was one of transition, but it was also an age of expansion and opportunity. The self-made yeoman or crown servant who could claw his way to the top — and stay there — could acquire enough land and influence to found a dynasty. The first quarries on Portland were starting to open. Manor houses not monasteries now provided Purbeck stone with a market. Every spring, a fleet of cogs and nefs set sail from Poole bound for the Newfoundland fisheries. Those that survived the crossing would return from the Banks in the autumn, each of them having landed as many as 250,000 cod and filled its holds with sealskin and whale blubber. As trade increased, so also did the market for Bridport's nets and ropes. Smuggling became commonplace. At Lyme Regis, flat-bottomed boats laden with 'fardels of linen and tuns of sweet wyne' plied to and fro between the Cobb and Cobb Gate.

Inland, sheep grazed the downs and cattle the water

meadows in the vales. Sherborne had survived the loss of its abbey and turned itself into the wealthiest town in the county. Broadcloth had left Dorchester nearly as prosperous, and all round it 'were sweet fields and spacious downs'. Some towns had reached the summit of their fortunes: Shaftesbury, Corfe Castle, Wareham. Melcombe Regis and Weymouth seemed doomed, but had a golden age still ahead of them. Others had begun to accept that they would always remain the mixture of market town and backwater that still typifies them today.

This book covers three centuries. Inevitably, much has been telescoped; much more omitted. At first glance it might even seem that the placid respectability of Dorset's present characterized its past. But here we are at the mercy of the artist and those who bought his work. Many of the illustrations in this book were originally sold as prints by the booksellers in the county. As such, their content reflects popular taste and the world of those who could afford them. Hardship and poverty rarely intrude. Even farming and rural life are all too often thought unworthy of the artist. Despite such faults, they cannot be replaced or improved and many are very rare. The delight and sense of discovery that stayed with me when searching for them is a tribute to the richness of Dorset's heritage. For they are its portrait, and in combination they mirror the changes that have shaped the Dorset we live in today.

# Acknowledgements

I am grateful to the following for allowing me permission to reproduce illustration in their possession: Dorset County Museum: *Illustration numbers*, 1, 2, 3, 4, 5, 6, 9, 16, 19, 24, 25, 26, 30, 31, 39, 43, 44, 45, 46, 47, 49, 50, 55, 64, 66, 67, 69, 70, 71, 76, 77, 81, 82, 85, 86, 90, 92, 93, 95, 96, 97, 98, 99, 102, 103, 106, 111, 113, 114, 119, 122, 125, 127, 131, 132, 133, 134. The Bridport Museum & Art Gallery: 74, 115, 116, 118. The British Library: 28, 33, 34, 35, 57, 75. (D. Burnett: 29, 58, 68.) The Dorset Military Museum, Dorchester: 65. The Guildhall Museum, Poole: 18, 100, 101, 104, 105. E.M. Jenkins: 117. Lyme Regis Museum: 72, 73, 79, 80, 120, 121, 123, 124. The National Museum of Wales: 23, 61. The Gerald Pitman Sherborne Pictorial Record Collection: 51, 52, 53. The Portland Museum: 91. The Priest's House Museum, Wimborne, 10, 11, 12, 48. The Shaftesbury Local History Museum: 13, 14, 15. The Sherborne Museum: 7, 130. Sherborne School: 32. Humphrey Stone: 8. The Tithe Barn Museum, Swanage: 88. The Victoria & Albert Museum: 56. The Wareham Pictorial Museum: 17, 60. The Weymouth Museum: 20, 21, 22, 27, 40, 42, 59, 62, 63, 78, 87, 89, 94, 107, 108, 109, 110, 112, 126, 128, 129. The Weymouth Public Library: 36, 37, 38, 41, 54, 83, 84.

Once again I am indebted to Roger Peers, Curator of the Dorset County Museum, for his support, encouragement and advice. I am also grateful to the following for their willingness to allow me to photograph the illustrations in this book and their invaluable help with the research: 'Skylark' Durston, Miss Marjorie Rogers (Sherborne Museum), Mrs. L. Pascall (Wareham Pictorial Museum), Mrs. J.E. Grainger (Shaftesbury Local History Museum), Miss H.M. Coles (Priest's House Museum, Wimborne), Miss Maureen Boddy and the staff of Weymouth Public Library, Gerald Pitman, John Sales (Bridport Museum), John Fowles (Lyme Regis Museum), Graham Smith and the staff of the Guildhall Museum, Poole, R.G.S. Avery (Tithe Barn Museum, Swanage), Jack West (Weymouth Museum), The Headmaster of Sherborne School, A.D. Childs (Sherborne School), Frank Clafton (Portland Museum), Major J. Wyllie (The Military Museum), and the staff of the County Records Office.

# Towns

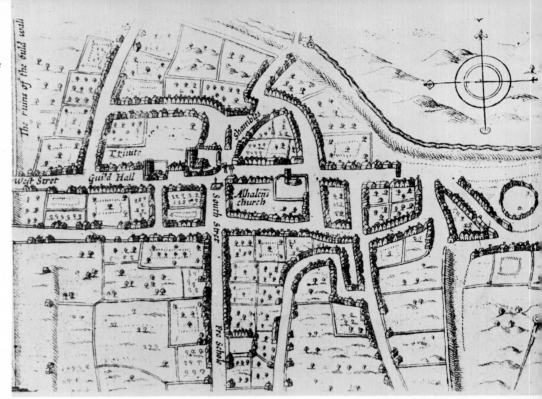

2. Dorchester from the east in the 1770s, showing Segar's Orchard and the fields that then ringed the town. By drowning the meadows from hatches on the Frome after hay making, cattle could be grazed until Christmas. It is worth noting that contemporary commentators thought little of the county's dairy produce: much of the butter was of such poor quality it was salted into tubs and supplied to the naval dockyard at Portsmouth.

3. Dorchester in 1610, three years before it was described as 'beautified with faire streets and many stately buildings'. Few of those buildings survive; that same year a fire broke out in a tallow chandler's shop. A shortage of water and the absence of many of the townsfolk gathering in the harvest hampered attempts to stop it spreading and 300 houses were destroyed. Note the livestock pound adjoining the London road and the large areas of open farm land inside the remains of the Roman wall.

4. Dorchester from Maumbury Rings in 1723; from a drawing by the antiquarian William Stukeley. The neolithic earthwork was adapted by the Romans as an amphitheatre, but when Stukeley visited it he 'saw all the area plowed up . . . and on one side stands the Gallows so that the top is much broken down with trampling of people to see executions'. It was here that the ill-fated Mary Channing was burnt for poisoning her husband in 1705 before a crowd of 10,000.

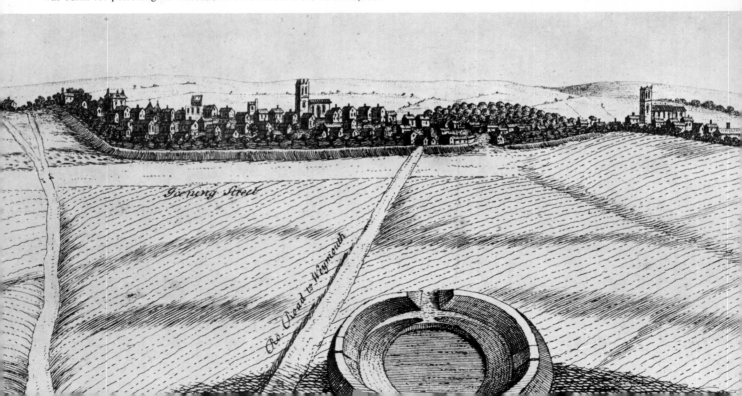

5, 6. Two views of High West Street, Dorchester, from Top o'Town in the 1830s. Although the slight change of angle does little to explain the differences, it is worth observing how one artist has chosen to emphasize the air of gentility that characterized 19th century Dorchester, whilst the other has portrayed it as a bustling market town. The uniformed solider was probably returning to the Marabout Barracks, built in 1795 for the Dorset Yeomanry.

7. Sherborne from the Slopes prior to the opening of the South Western Railway in 1860.

8. A view of Bridport from Allington Hill in the 1830s. Bridport owed its growth to flax and hemp, the two crops used in the manufacture of ropes, netting and marine cordage. The wide streets remain evidence of the covered rope walks that used to extend outwards from the houses.

9. The Market Place, Blandford, in about 1840, little more than a century after the great fire of 1731 which virtually destroyed the town. The fire, the fourth in 150 years, began in a tallow chandler's shop, was fanned by a brisk north westerly wind, and quickly engulfed the town's three fire-engines. A grocery containing a stock of gunpowder then exploded, adding to the confusion. The wind shifted, and continued doing so until the flames had reached the neighbouring villages of Bryanston and Blandford St. Mary and all but three houses in the town had been destroyed. Efforts to control the blaze were made worse by a smallpox epidemic, and many of the sick were placed under the arches of the bridge over the Stour.

10. Wimborne and the Minster from an incorrectly placed south bank of the Stour in 1787, or perhaps a now non-existent pond in The Leaze.

11. Wimborne from Cole Hill in the 1850s. The parish of Colehill was not created until 1894 and most of the fields visible in the foreground have since been built over.

12. West Borough, Wimborne, in about 1840; a year when that one street could boast 5 milliners, 3 inns, a chimney sweep, 3 schools, a wheelwright, 3 blacksmiths, a shipping and emigration agent, a coach painter, 2 shoemakers and 3 livery stables. Missing is the conduit that once ran from Walford Bridge providing water for fire-fighting and street cleaning.

14. Shaftesbury High Street in 1840. The water cart outside St. Peter's Church is a reminder of a shortage that permanently troubled the townsfolk, the lack of water. Many houses had shoots for catching rain-water from their roofs, but most water had to be brought in, either from springs at Cann, a conduit at the foot of Castle Hill, or from wells near Motcombe. In Motcombe's case, the village was rewarded by an annual payment of a raw calf's head, a pair of gloves, a gallon of beer and two 1d loaves. The water was sold by carriers, at prices ranging from a farthing for a bucketful to 2d a horse load.

13. Shaftesbury in 1795, looking north towards Gold Hill and St. Peter's Church. The town originally owed its 'flourishing condition' to its abbey, 12 churches and 3 mints. Even in the late 18th century it remained an important market town, attracting trade from as far afield as Devizes. Cattle and pigs were sold on Gold Hill; there were butter, fish, cheese and poultry crosses, as well as two dozen inns where the thirsty could seek refuge from the din. Note the curious carriage road running across Park Hill.

15. The Commons, Shaftesbury, in 1850. The Grosvenor Arms dates from about 1800. For a small payment Rutter's Printing Office could obtain books, newspapers and the 'very latest Intelligence by post-chaise direct from the Angel, St. Clements', London, if God permits' within two days.

18. The Poole Exhibition of works of Industry & Art, held in the Guildhall in 1854. The 'works' included paintings, furniture, clocks, china, needlework, fossils and fire-arms — amongst them two cannons captured by Nelson at the Battle of Copenhagen. It seems the Exhibition was a success. According to the local paper, 'countless multitudes and enthusiastic crowds thronged the Glorious concourse proving Britannia's Majesty'.

⌂ 16. The bridge over the Frome, Wareham, in the late 18th century, showing Lady St. Mary Church before the replacement of the Saxon nave in 1841. The town's importance as a port had long since declined, mainly due to silting in the river, an increase in the size of shipping and competition from Poole. What was once Abbot's Quay, to the left of the bridge, is now shown occupied by tenements.

▽ 17. The junction of Wareham's four main streets in the 1840s, looking along North Street. To the left is the Red Lion Hotel; to the right, and on the site of a medieval church, the Town Hall of 1768 but since rebuilt.

19. The works at East Quay, Hamworthy, of the Patent Architectural Pottery Co., a year after they opened in 1854. The company was the first of the Poole potteries and made mouldings, glazed bricks and ornamental tiles. It was bought out in 1895 by Jesse Carter, founder of Poole Pottery. Carter paid £2,000 for the factory, 5 cottages and 56 building plots.

20. Shipping at anchor in Weymouth in 1827. The cutter on the left can be distinguished by its flag as a packet ship. A regular packet service between Weymouth and the Channel Islands had first been established in 1794, the packets carrying passengers as well as mail but no freight. Fares ranged from £1 for a 'gentleman' to 15/- for a servant. 1827 was the first year in which a paddle steamer made the crossing to Jersey.

21. The *Flamer* entering Weymouth in about 1835. The 165 ton paddle-steamer was built in 1831. Two years later a wave carried away the deck gear and ship's boat, flooding the cabin and stranding the passengers on the companion way. The steamer was renamed the *Fearless*, but the change of name had little effect on its seaworthiness and it was withdrawn from service in 1839. It ended its days employed in minor dockyard duties for the Navy. The Channel Islands packet service was transferred to Southampton in 1845.

29. A fisherman shrimping on the beach between Charmouth and Lyme Regis in about 1810, engraved from a drawing by J.M.W. Turner.

28. Seine netting for mackerel off Chesil Beach in 1791. Fish were caught off the Beach between March and midsummer, providing seasonal employment in all the coastal villages. A watchman was posted on Chapel Hill above Abbotsbury to spot the shoals whilst the crews of the boats waited 'in a convenient cottage with a hogshead of cider'. In 10 days in 1791 so many fish were taken that the price dropped to 1/- per 30 hundredweight wagon load. A more usual price was 1d a 100. The nets were 500 foot long and 40 foot deep and as many as 40,000 fish might be landed in a single draught. The panniers over the pack-horse were known locally as 'dorsers'.

30. Poole in the late 18th century, looking towards Little Quay from Hamworthy. Proximity to the sea dominated Poole's growth and by 1600 it was a Port of the Staple whose imports included fish, salt, resin and oil. The establishment of the trade with Newfoundland added to Poole's prosperity and the private wharfs along the waterfront were reclaimed in order to create the Little Quay and a fish market. By 1670 the Newfoundland trade employed a total of 300 ships and the Fish Street warehouses were crammed with cod and barrels of cod oil, seal skins and whale blubber: 'a great nuisance to ye inhabitants by reason of ye stench'.

31. (Overleaf) Poole waterfront and the Great Quay in the 1850s. Although the Newfoundland trade was already in decline, 'the capacity and convenience of its quays; the large, airy and spacious stores, affording facilities for the warehousing of goods at trifling expense; the superior accommodation provided for building, repairing, chaulking or careening ships', made Poole 'a most desirable place of commercial resort'. At the height of the town's prosperity, 1,500 tons of goods were being unloaded a week and the Channel was often so crowded with shipping 'that it was possible to cross the harbour on foot all the way'.

**32.** The Conduit, and the corner of Cheap Street and Long Street, Sherborne, in the 1820s.
Originally situated in the abbey cloisters, the Conduit was moved to the Parade in the 16th century to
pipe water to the School and part of the town. Shortly after this print was published it was partially
bricked up and let as a reading room. By the end of the century it had seen service as the town lock-
up, a penny bank and a depot for stuffing pillows.

33,34. A Portland quarryman with his tools in about 1790.

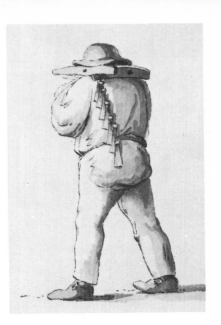

35. Quarrymen moving stone on Portland in about 1790. Note the brake horses at the rear and the smaller stone mounted on a sledge. In 1804 a visiting clergyman observed that on the downhill journey to the loading piers the horses 'squat down on their haunches and suffer themselves to be dragged for many yards, struggling with all their strength against the weight that forces them forwards'. The Rev. Skinner also realized that so arduous a journey could be ended by 'the simple construction of a railroad'. The Merchants' Railway opened in 1826.

36. Stonecutters preparing to lever a stone on to a trundle or cart in a Purbeck quarry in the late 18th century; a period when some 50,000 tons of marble were being shipped from Swanage a year.

Royal Seaside

37. *(Overleaf)* On July 8th 1789, whilst staying with his brother at Weymouth and in hope of improving his health, George III took his first bathe in the sea. Sea-bathing was already fashionable, but the king's patronage helped change recreational habits more profoundly than at any time in their history. 'The King Bathes', announced the cartoon by John Nixon on the preceding page, 'and with great success. A machine follows the Royal one into the sea, filled with fiddlers, who play God Save the King as His Majesty takes his plunge!' George III last stayed in Weymouth in 1805, the following year his doctors thought him too mad to risk the journey from Windsor.

38. George III on the Esplanade at Weymouth in 1797, a cartoon by Gillray. The words of a contemporary visitor to the town seem more than apt: 'The concourse of fashionable company at this place during the height of the season is very great, and affords a picture both highly interesting and amusing'.

39. George III visiting Dorchester Goal in 1792, 2 years after the old prison at the foot of East Street was abandoned and the County Goal built on its present site. The new goal had 88 cells as well as a brewery and debtors' day rooms. New admissions were shaved, bathed and fumigated. Their basic diet was beer, bread, broth and 9d worth of meat a week (scrag was about 3d a lb). During his visit, the king paid a mason's debts and ordered that he be freed.

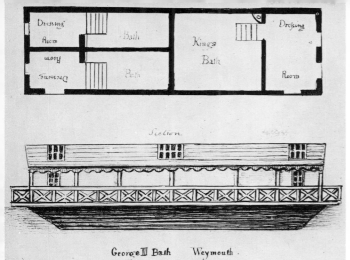

George III Bath    Weymouth.

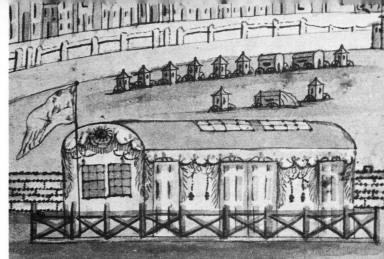

**41,42.** A plan and sketch of the King's Bath. The interior of the Bath was left open to the sea so that the king could swim in private.

▷ **43.** The interior of the King's Bath showing Princesses Charlotte, Elizabeth and Augusta. This illustration was entitled "The Royal Bathers or Maids in their Proper Element" and the commentary beneath it went on to compare the royal princesses to fish and debate how best they might be caught by a potential suitor. 'When Sweet Eliza takes a dip', wrote a contemporary poetaster of Princess Elizabeth, 'I envy Neptune's peeping'.

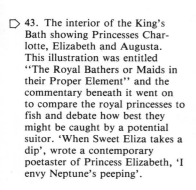

◁ **40.** "*A Royal Salute to the King on the Esplanade at Weymouth*". The lady shown is thought to be Lady Reed, a well-known eccentric who is supposed to have kept monkeys in her old age — even insisting that they sleep in her bed.

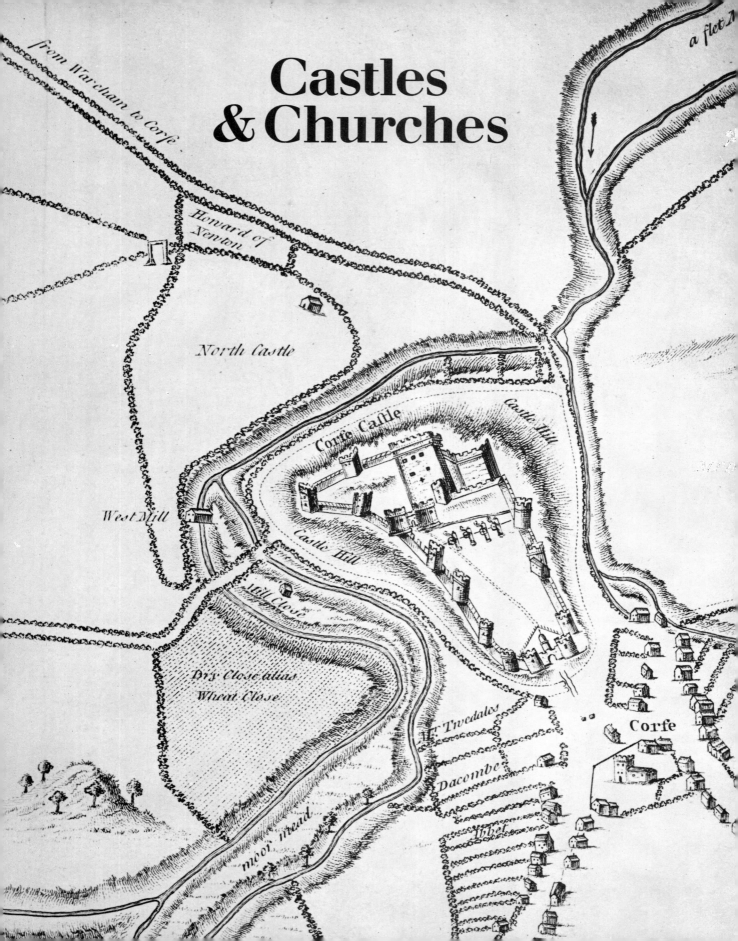

# Castles
# & Churches

from Wareham to Corfe

Howard of Newton

North Castle

Corfe Castle

Castle Hill

West Mill

Castle Hill

Mill Close

Dry Close alias
Wheat Close

moor mead

Mr Tivedales

Dacombe

Abbot

Corfe

a flet M

44. A section of Ralph Treswell's survey of Corfe Castle in 1585. Despite its weekly market, borough status and importance to the Purbeck stone trade, the town itself was no larger than many a village. Sixty years later, during the siege of the castle, the lead was stripped from the church roof to make bullets and powder and shot were stored in the organ pipes.

45, 46. Two engravings showing Corfe Castle before and after its deliberate destruction in 1647. The lower illustration dates from 1843, by which time the first of numerous legends had gathered round the story of Lady Bankes's defence of the castle during the Civil War and its final capture by Parliament. The cost of demolishing the walls and blowing up the towers was so great that an additional levy was added to the county rates.

47. St. Martin's Chapel, Wareham, in the 18th century. According to legend it was built in 698 by St. Adhelm whilst prevented by gales from crossing the Channel. It was disused by 1736 and employed to shelter the homeless after the fire of 1762. The Chapel was re-dedicated in 1936 and contains Kennington's effigy of T.E. Lawrence, Lawrence of Arabia.

48. The Minster Church of St. Cuthberga, Wimborne, in the 1820s, a view from the High Street.

49. Lulworth Castle in about 1770. After the purchase of the late 16th century castle by Humphrey Weld in 1641 it was to remain the family home of the Welds until the fire of 1929 which completely gutted the interior.

50. Branksea, or Brownsea Castle, in the 1850s. Brownsea Island now belongs to the National Trust, but its earlier proprietors include Colonel Waugh and the mad William Benson whose sudden distaste for books led to all those in the castle being burnt in bonfires on the beach. Waugh was its owner in the 1850s, having paid £13,000 for the Island on the strength of a geologist's report suggesting that large deposits of China clay lay beneath it. He built a pier, church, clock tower, stables and school, made two lakes and reclaimed what is now known as the 'Lagoon'. The geologist's report proved illusory. When it was finally discovered that the clay was only adequate for the manufacture of drain pipes, Waugh and his wife fled to Spain, leaving debts of £250,000.

51, 52. Two views of the interior of the Abbey Church of St. Mary, Sherborne, before the restoration began in 1849.

**53.** Boys at Sherborne School in the Bell Court in about 1845, nearly 300 years after the school's foundation as a Free Grammar School. Its history was chequered, its growth erratic: in the 15 years before 1850 numbers fell from 127 boys to 40 boys and 2 masters. The daily routine was as follows: 7 a.m. — prayers and Greek grammar, 8.15 — prayers and breakfast, 9.15 to 12.00 — Xenophon, 2.15 to 5.00 — Virgil and Latin grammar, 7.30 — exercises and Greek. The boys on the right are playing 'top-whipping'.

**54.** Portland Castle in the early 19th century. The castle was built by Henry VIII in about 1540 as part of a coastal defence system. Within a century the roof timbers above the gun-room were rotting and by 1707 it was in virtual ruins. It has recently been restored, and was actually rented out as a private house for much of the 19th century.

55. The Great Batteries on the Nothe, Weymouth, during the construction of Portland Breakwater in the 1850s. The Breakwater was originally conceived in response to the new fortress at Cherbourg, and was intended to provide a sheltered deep water anchorage for the larger ships then beginning to be built by the Navy. By the date of its initial completion in 1872 it had used 6 million tons of stone and cost double its original estimate — a fact which doubtless explains why the *Poole & Dorsetshire Herald*, which had called it 'one of those national acts of charity to all men' when it was started, ended up by damning it as a 'woeful list of hideous failure and costly mismanagement'.

56. The drawing by Phillip Brannon on which the preceding engraving was based. Note the deletions and additions made by the engraver.

57. A thatched privy outside the entrance to the ruins of Abbotsbury Abbey, a drawing by Samuel Hieronymus Grimm dated 1790.

59. John Love, Weymouth book and print seller, who died aged 41 in 1793 when he weighed 26 stone and was reputedly 'the most remarkable man in all England for his weight and corpulence'. After being apprenticed to the engraver William Ryland (later hung for forgery), Love set up in Weymouth when the town first became fashionable. Even as a young man 'his weight and bulk were the astonishment of all beholders', but claims that he was the fattest man in England are undoubtedly false. Possible rivals for the title must include a Mr. Bowe from near Wimborne, who weighed 34 stone and died after downing a gallon of cider in the belief that it would cure his gout.

58. Abbotsbury Abbey from the north in 1733, showing the Great Barn and the Swannery beyond.

60. John Hutchins (1698-1773), rector of Holy Trinity, Wareham, and author of the monumental *History & Antiquities of the County of Dorset*; a labour of such accuracy, detail and scholarship that it still remains the standard work on the county. The manuscript was nearly engulfed by the fire that swept Wareham in 1762 and owes its survival to his wife. 'The Winter of Life . . . is coming on', he wrote afterwards, badly shaken but not aware that although he would finish his history he would not live to see its final publication in 1774.

61. Mary Anning (1799-1847) searching for fossils near Lyme Regis; a light-hearted and affectionate sketch by Henry De la Beche — later to be knighted and made President of the Geological Society. Mary Anning owed her friendship with De la Beche to her discovery, when still a child, of part of the fossilized remains of an extinct marine animal called an Ichthyosaur. The discovery provided her with an occupation (she used to sell the specimens she found) and turned her into Lyme's most celebrated resident.

62. A convict in his cell in Portland Prison. The prison opened in 1848 and was regarded as an important penal experiment for men sentenced to transportation. Considerable freedoms could be won by those who behaved well when they were finally sent to the Colonies. There were 700 cells, each was 7 foot by 4 foot and divided from its neighbours by a corrugated iron partition.

63. Convicts at Portland Prison at work in the quarries. Most were sentenced to either 7 or 10 years transportation, usually for theft. When Prince Albert visited Portland and asked that one of the convicts be pardoned, 'the effect on the poor fellow was very touching. He at first danced for joy, and finally, overpowered by his emotions, fell on the ground'. The prison closed in 1921 and has since re-opened as a Borstal Institution.

64. "A Windy Day", a drawing by the poet William Barnes (1801-1886). Barnes's fame as the 'Dorset Poet' has tended to overshadow his other achievements. He began drawing and engraving when a solicitor's engrossing clerk in Dorchester, later even advertising for commissions — hence: 'Visiting Cards, Bill-Heads, etc, engraved on copper, in every variety of style. Ornamental designs for printers, on wood. Likenesses taken in pencil, from 7/6d to 10/6d each'.

65. Members of Princess Victoria's Regiment of Dorset Yeomanry Cavalry in about 1835. The Regiment, later the Queen's Own Dorset Yeomanry, was founded in 1794 to strengthen the Militia when invasion by the French seemed likely. After Waterloo it gradually disbanded, but was reformed in the 1830s to counter civil disorder and the agricultural riots. An early report by the regimental doctor advised the drinking of plenty of 'good malted liquor', even suggesting that the addition of 'brandy, rum or gin in cold weather might be expedient'. He also stated that 'Bread, meat and potatoes give and preserve robust muscular strength. Greens and fruits should be used sparingly, lest they produce fluxes'.

66, 67. Two engravings showing the raid by smugglers on Poole Customs House in October 1747 and the later death of an excise officer. A revenue cutter had intercepted smugglers and impounded 2 tons of tea and 40 casks of brandy. High Kingsmill, leader of the notorious 'Hawkhurst Gang' from Kent, and 60 of his men attacked the Customs House and escaped with the contraband..They were later recognized by a cobbler, who together with an excise officer set out for Chichester to lay information against the smugglers. They never arrived. They were taken from their beds in a wayside inn, Chater was buried alive and the excise officer thrown down a well: 'but even then life lingered in his poor mangled body, and so, by way of completing their fiendish job, the smugglers threw down large stones and pieces of timber, until every sign of life was hushed'. The members of the Gang were later caught and hung, but Kingsmill did not repent. Prior to his hanging, he demanded wine, tobacco and pipes, 'as I am determined to live well the short time I have to be in this world'.

68. Deer hunters on Cranborne Chase in about 1740, wearing their traditional Cap and Jack. The Cap was made of straw bound with split bramble; the Jack, or coat, out of quilted canvas that gave protection against keepers' quarter-staffs. Pitched battles between keepers and poachers were once common on the Chase. On one occasion, when hunters were disturbed, 'and making use of their old phrase, Stand Firm, my Boys, and cock 'em!, a violent battle ensued. The hunters were desperately wounded, and lie dangerous, some with the loss of their legs, others with their arms broke; the keepers shared almost the same fate, but were beat unmercilessly'.

69. Henry Hastings, squire of Woodlands near Wimborne. To do justice to Hastings is almost impossible, but the portrait of him by Antony Ashley Cooper (later 1st Earl of Shaftesbury) delightfully evokes one of Dorset's most remarkable eccentrics. Hastings died in 1650 aged 99 after a life spent fishing, coursing, hawking and hunting — 'but what he borrowed to caress his neighbours' wives and daughters'. Despite such excesses, his popularity was immense, his hospitality celebrated. Those who entered his house found a hall strewn with marrow bones, hawks on their perches, fox skins on the walls, kittens in every chair and dogs sprawled by the fire. At one end was a table laden with oysters — for he ate Poole oysters twice a day — and a collection of hats, all with their crowns thrust in so as to hold a dozen pheasant eggs. Beyond the hall was the chapel, its pulpit his larder 'never wanting for a cold chine of beef, venison pasty, gammon of bacon, or a great apple pie'. Even aged ninety Hastings could mount a horse unaided, and 'until past fourscore he rode to the death of a stag as well as any'.

# Shipwrecks

70. *(Overleaf)* An unidentified shipwreck in Worbarrow Bay, circa 1800.

71. The wreck of the *Halsewell* off Seacombe Cliff near Winspit in 1786. The ship was an East Indiaman outward bound for Bombay when she began shipping water. When the wind rose, the captain turned for Studland Bay. In the early hours of January 6th the *Halsewell* struck the cliff 'with such violence, a shriek of horror burst at one instant from every quarter of the ship'. By dawn she had broken in two. The survivors took shelter in a cave at the foot of the cliff, from where they were eventually rescued. Out of a complement of 240, there were 74 survivors. The illustration shows Captain Pierce, his 2 daughters, 2 nieces and '3 other beautiful young ladies, clinging round their captain for protection'.

72, 73. The London trader the *Unity* being driven ashore at Lyme Regis during the Great Storm of November 1824. The lower illustration shows the *Unity* being washed under the cliffs and a Captain Benett about to be lowered to the ship in a successful attempt to rescue the master. One member of the crew fell from the rigging, but lived, whilst the bruised and exhausted second seaman and ship's boy had to be cut from the rigging and dragged ashore. The *Unity* was later relaunched. Benett was awarded the Gold Medal of the newly formed Royal National Institute for the Preservation of Life from Shipwreck (now the R.N.L.I.), and Lyme was provided with a life saving mortar so heavy it could not be moved from the Cobb. The lower illustration is an example of Carter Galpin's 'black lead process'.

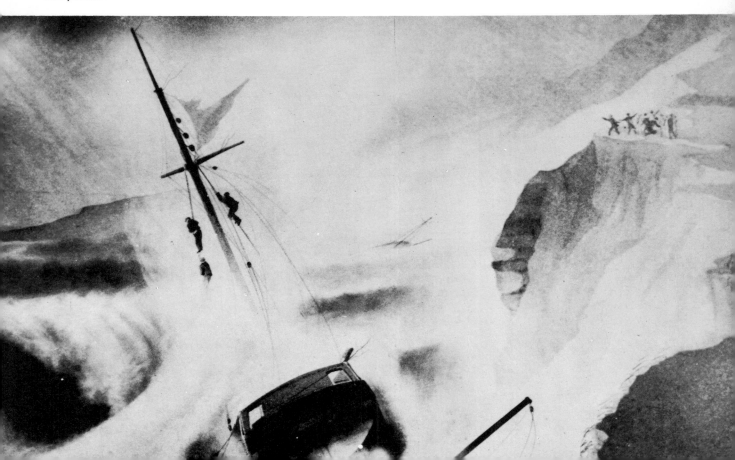

74. Charles Sturt, M.P. for Bridport, owner of both Brownsea Island and Crichel House, awaiting rescue after capsizing off Portland in 1800. Sturt had lashed himself in his boat, 'as he expected to drift a corpse on shore. All which time several large Gannets were hovering close to him, anticipating their prey'. He was eventually rescued by a military transport and was 'welcomed by the Sailors with that honest Joy which so honourably distinguishes the heart of the British Tar'.

75. The Lower Lighthouse, Portland, shortly after its construction in 1789. Both the Upper and Lower lighthouses were originally built in 1716, but their coal fired lights were feeble and irregularly lit. The replacement Lower lighthouse stood 63 feet high and had 6 oil-fired lamps. Above the doorway an inscription read: 'For the Direction and Comfort of Navigators, the Benefit & Security of Commerce, and a lasting Memorial of British Hospitality to all Nations'. Both lighthouses were replaced by the existing lighthouse in 1906 and the Lower house is now a Bird Observatory.

76. Turner's dramatic but romantic interpretation of a shipwreck at West Bay, Bridport, in the early 19th century.

77. Attempts to take off survivors from the wreck of the *Earl of Abergavenny* in February 1805. The *Earl of Abergavenny* was sailing in convoy when she settled at low tide on the Shambles. Calm gave way to panic when the wind lifted and it was discovered that the merchantman was shipping water. Finally the ship slipped off the shoal and sank in 12 fathoms. The survivors climbed the rigging, but as night fell and the waves began breaking over the masts many fell and were drowned. The captain, brother of the poet Wordsworth, and about 300 others died in the disaster.

78. The 'ingenious Mr. Tomkins' and his divers trying to salvage some of the £70,000 reputed to be on board the *Earl of Abergavenny* when she sank. The wreck remained a navigational hazard until it was broken up by the Navy in the 1920s.

# Pleasures & Pastimes

79. *(Overleaf)*" Hydromania! or a 'Touch of the Sub-Lyme and Beautiful' — The Beach at Lyme Regis'', a perhaps unique engraving published in 1819 from a cartoon by Cruikshank. Lyme first became fashionable in the 1760s when the sick came to it in search of health and 'brought beauty and elegance in their train'. A contemporary treatise on sea-bathing declared that 'to bathe late (especially in hot weather) will occasion great depression of the spirits. Perfect repose of body and serenity of mind are necessary to promote the purpose of this great remedy. Bathers then find their spirits exhilarated and feel a universal glow through the system'.

80. Madeira Cottages and the remains of West Fort, Lyme Regis, a detail from a drawing by Captain Marryat, author of *Mr. Midshipman Easy* and *The Children of the New Forest*.

82, 83. Blandford Races in 1818 (the wrestling bout in the lower illustration was one of the many regular attractions during the July races). The races were held on Monkton Down, now occupied by Blandford Camp. They are first mentioned in 1603 and were extinct by the 1850s. The main race was the Dorsetshire Gold Cup, worth a 100 guineas and run over 4 miles.

83. Ladies of fashion in the Assembly Rooms, Weymouth, in 1774, two years after the Rooms first opened. They were large enough to allow '100 couples to dance with ease and pleasure', and were governed by a formidable list or rules. Men in boots and women in riding habit were banned. Women were even forbidden to wear coloured gloves when dancing.

84. A cartoon by Gillray showing Weymouth Esplanade in 1810, a year in which it cost 1/6d to hire a bathing machine, umbrella, a guide and bathing dresses. Gossip thrived as Weymouth grew more fashionable. By 1810 even the local newspaper felt able to announce that the 'celebrated Mrs.-W, whose amours are renowned, is here without a paramour, or even a single servant. Her amours have just produced a little girl'.

85. A barrow at Shapwick, near Sturminster Marshall, after its excavation in 1838. Finds included a probably Bronze Age cremation, but as the barrow stood close to the Stour digging had to cease when it began filling with water. The excavator, the then curate of Sturminster Marshall, Charles Wools, later commemorated the dig by writing *The Barrow Diggers; a Dialogue in Imitation of the Grave Diggers in Hamlet*, a mixture of farce and serious scholarship.

86. Damory Oak, Blandford, in 1747. The oak stood at the east end of the town and served as an inn capable of holding 20 occupants. It had a 68 foot circumference, and the interior was 15 foot wide and 17 foot high. It was sold standing for £14 in 1755 and felled for fire-wood.

87. The west end of Weymouth Esplanade in 1821, showing the Nothe and Devonshire Buildings.

88. Swanage in the 1850s, looking west along the Parade. Swanage's career as a port began in the 18th century and ended in 1887 with the arrival of the railway. At one point an attempt was made to start a herring fishery, but when Charles Kingsley stayed in the town it was still untouched by the changes that were to follow. 'A pleasanter spot for sea-bathing is not to be found', he wrote, 'and all that is wanted to make it famous is houses into which visitors can put their heads for the night'. To the left can be seen the Royal Victoria Hotel, named after Princess Victoria's visit in 1835.

89. Luce's Hotel and the Esplande, Weymouth, in 1842; from a drawing by Henry Burns who also drew the ascent of the *Albion* balloon (see no. 126). Burns later emigrated to Australia and went mad, ending his days in Melbourne Asylum.

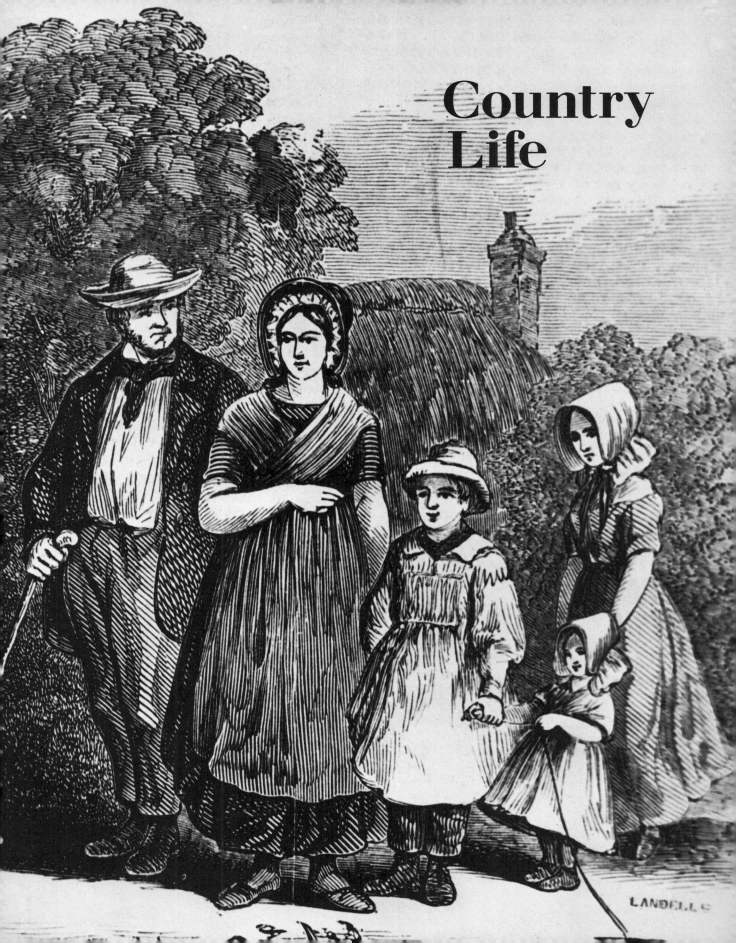

# Country
# Life

90. *(Overleaf)* A group of Dorset labourers in 1846. This illustration, and numbers 92 & 96, are taken from an article in the *Illustrated London News* about the plight of agricultural workers in the county.

92. Winterborne Whitchurch in 1846, another illustration from the article on conditions in rural Dorset in the *Illustrated London News*. Describing the village, it said, 'The first feature which attracts the stranger is the total want of cleanliness. A stream, composed of the matter which continually escapes from pigsties and other receptacles of filth, meanders down every street . . . so as to create wonder that the place is not the continual abode of pestilence'. The magazine concluded that the main causes of poverty in the county were 'the apathy and indifference of the landed proprietor and the grasping closefisted policy of the farmer'. In 1850 the Dorset agricultural worker's basic diet of barley bread, skim milk, cheese and potatoes was worse than that of a convict on Portland.

91. Boys selling wheatears, or 'snalters', taken from stone traps in the street at Weston, Portland, in 1802; one of a series of paintings by J.W. Upham commissioned by John Penn — seen here in the foreground in the uniform of the Royal Portland Legion. Wheatears characteristically run along the ground and take refuge in small holes. Using horsehair snares placed in the hollow centre of stone cairns, boys could catch up to 400 birds a day during the harvest months. The birds sold for 3d a dozen and were cooked strung on twigs with vine leaves.

93. Abbotsbury from the east in the early 19th century, a view of the village and Chapel Hill seen from a field called Broad Close.

94. Upwey in 1818, a view of the village that the intervening years have done little to modify.

95. Sheep being driven along the Bridport road, Dorchester, in the 1850s. Sheep were the mainstay of Dorset agriculture. In 1793 it was estimated that there were 800,000 in the county and that 150,000 were sold annually to supply external markets. By then the pure-bred Dorset Horn was already growing scarce, for it had been crossed with other breeds and largely replaced by the Dorset Down, a more economical sheep that required less pasture. Dorset's third indigenous sheep was the Portland, a small and now rare sheep of characteristic flavour.

96. The interior of a Stourpaine cottage, 1846. A report by the Poor Law Commissioners into conditions in Stourpaine found disease, prostitution, child labour and malnutrition. In one case the 3 beds in a single room cottage were occupied by a husband and wife and their 2 babies, their 3 daughters, and the 4 eldest boys. The writer in the *Illustrated London News* stated when visiting the village that the view through 'an open door, which reveals a mud floor and the usual heap of squalid half-clothed children rolling upon it, serves to remind you that you are in Dorsetshire'.

97. Bryanston House in 1714, showing the formal gardens and the Stour in the foreground. It was replaced in 1778 by a new house designed by James Wyatt. A century later, when Lord Portman built the existing Bryanston House, Wyatt's house was demolished and a church built on the site.

98. Villagers driving away the 'Shapwick Monster'. In 1841 a travelling fishmonger bound for Blandford accidentally dropped a crab near Shapwick. The villagers, who had never seen a crab before and thought it to be a form of monster, first fortified themselves with beer and then attempted to drive it away with sticks and pitchforks. The fishmonger returned in search of his lost crab and casually put it back in his basket:

    'Amazement seized the admiring crowd,
    And this their fears expressed aloud,
    ''Take Care! — He'll Bite! — You've caught the Devil!'' '

For years afterwards no one from Shapwick could visit the fishmongers' stalls at the local markets without being mocked and reminded of the 'Monster'.


99. Woodbury Hill, Bere Regis; from a drawing by Stukeley in 1724. The Hill was the site of Dorset's largest fair, held for 5 days from September 18th and of such importance that 'Woodbury Day' was used for dating manorial documents. Goods sold included livestock, hops, cheeses, cloth and haberdashery. Court records contain many charges brought against the cut-purses and tricksters who regarded the fair as a potential source of revenue.

# Ports & Harbours

100. *(Overleaf)* Poole Quay in 1833. A portion of Poole's wealth was derived from the oyster beds in the harbour, originally formed by Channel Island oysters that had been thrown overboard. By the end of the 17th century Poole oysters were being pickled and barrelled and sent as far afield as the West Indies. By the 1830s new beds were being dredged and oysters carried to creeks at the mouth of the Thames where they were fattened for the London market. This illustration may evoke Poole's bustle, but it conceals the poverty once rife in the back-street brothels, taverns, and sailors' slum tenements.

101. 'A Prospect of the Town of Poole from the West End of Branksea Island' in the 17th century. The Key reads: A — Litchet Beacon, B — Wimborne Road, D — Pergin's Island, E — Upton, F — Oyster Bank, G — Ham & Ham Quay, H — Rope Walk, I — Quays, K — Heckford, L — Parkstone, M — Sturminster Road. The windmill on Baiter, where the gallows stood and the victims of the Black Death were buried, is first mentioned in 1542 when the town was granted the right 'to make, frame and set up . . . one good and sufficient windmill'.

The map contains the following place names and labels:

Longflete. Cantorde Launde[?]
South Lochiot
Byckford
Hamworthy
Poole
Parkston
The Mynes
Holton
Arnpaynb
Brunckley
Koſworth
Arne
Shepstall
Furley Inſul
Brunckley east
North haven point
St Elins Inſul
Gurie Orde
Cake Orde
Red Orde
Hlakepoole
Sleps
Newton
VibOwn
Godins
Philps
Brownds

102. A map of Poole Harbour in 1585. In its early history the Harbour was plagued by pirates who hid and victualled their ships in its creeks. In 1598 Brownsea was described as 'only a support for pirates to furnish their boats'. Records mention that 'pirates have cut down the gallows where the pirate was hanged at Studland'. In 1638 Algerian pirates entered the Harbour and pillaged Poole. A naval survey written at the end of the century concluded that 'the shoals are very large and the channels very crooked. There are few vessels that will venture into it when they can choose to do otherwise'. Note the cartographer's difficulty in drawing South Haven Point, then a sand bar of uncertain shape.

103. Poole and the Harbour from Constitution Hill in 1823.

104. Looking across at the Great Quay, Poole, from Hamworthy in about 1840.

105. The *Sylph* entering Leghorn, Italy, in 1855. The *Sylph* was a Poole built schooner that carried dried Newfoundland cod across the Atlantic for sale in Spain, Portugal or Italy. After leaving Leghorn it would have returned to Poole, taking on supplies and equipment for the fisheries before again making the voyage to Newfoundland.

◇ 106. The 'swivel method' bridge between Poole and Hamworthy in 1855. Prior to the bridge's construction in 1837, Hamworthy was reached by a ferry — at one point leased from the corporation for an annual rent of 2 capons.

▷ 107. Weymouth bridge in 1820. Unlike all previous bridges, that of 1770 was built opposite St. Nicholas Street in an attempt to enlarge the harbour. It was disliked by the townsfolk and restored to its traditional site when it was replaced in 1824 by the town's first stone bridge.

108, 109. Two views of Weymouth in about 1790. Note how the sea and Backwater came close to meeting at the Narrows (they actually did so on the night of the Great Storm in 1824). In the mid-18th century the foreshore was known as the Mixen and regarded as the back of town, a place for rubbish and 'houses of easement'. The canopies, or 'umbrellas', on the bathing machines in the bottom illustration have been lowered to provide privacy for the bathers.

110. The Marine Hotel, Weymouth, during a storm in 1802. On February 2nd a brig laden with fruit was driven ashore during a gale. The crew was rescued, but the cargo of oranges and lemons 'became a prey to plunders more merciless than the wind and waves'. During the storm — perhaps the one illustrated — the quay and adjacent streets were flooded and many bathing machines were destroyed.

111. Weymouth in 1850. A century earlier the owner of Charlotte Row tried to give half of it away — and failed. By 1850 the houses along the Esplanade were the most valuable town houses in Dorset.

112. A view of Swanage and the Bay, from near Peveril Point, in 1823.

113. Custom House Quay and Weymouth harbour in 1827. More than 400 ships a year were then docking in the harbour and the port had the right to warehouse certain bonded goods — amongst which were rice, brandy, tobacco and wine.

114. Swanage in the 1850s. By then William Morton Pitt had all but completed the town's transformation from port and fishing village into resort, opening Billiard and Coffee Rooms and planning a rail link with the pier head to speed the shipping of Purbeck stone.

115. West Bay, Bridport, in 1825. To be strictly accurate it was still Bridport Harbour, for the name West Bay was provided for the convenience of the Great Western Railway when the railway was extended to the harbour in 1884 and they wanted to distinguish it from the town. Bridport Harbour was built in the 18th century by diverting the River Brit and building wharfs and piers. Initially both piers consisted of oak piles, but by 1825 they had been rebuilt in stone and vessels entering the harbour were hauled up the channel by capstans.

116, 117. Two views of West Bay in the early 19th century. Note the sailing boat emerging from between the piers in the lower illustration. The harbour was originally built to assist the Bridport net and rope industry, but a glance at contemporary court records would seem to suggest that smuggling was the main occupation of its residents.

116. The 1460 ton *Speedy*, the largest ship built at Bridport, and, at the date of its launching in 1853, the largest ever built in Dorset. The *Speedy* was designed as a packet clipper to serve the Australia run and was 202 feet in length. It took several attempts to launch her and for two weeks she sat firmly aground in the harbour awaiting the next spring-tide.

119. Seatown from Golden Cap in 1723. The squares marked "B" on the west side of the river mouth were salt-pans. Salt- making in Dorset is first mentioned in Domesday and by the 15th century it was being exported to France. The discovery of salt mines in Cheshire led to the collapse of the market. By the date of Stukeley's drawing its manufacture in Dorset was all but over.

120. Lyme Regis and the Cobb, a detail from a map of the Dorset Coast made in 1539 when invasion by the French seemed imminent; note the warning beacon. The Cobb is first mentioned in 1294, but the town's growth had accelerated with the closure of the harbour at Axmouth by a cliff-fall in the 12th century. Apart from attracting trade and offering shelter to shipping crossing Lyme Bay, the Cobb protected the town from the prevailing south-westerlies.

121. The Cobb, Lyme Regis, in 1723; engraved from a drawing by Stukeley that shows Ferrye's Island and the Cobb before it was connected to the land in 1756. Note that the boulders and oak piles that composed the Elizabethan Cobb had by then been replaced.

122. Gun Cliff, Lyme Regis, in 1832. The artist, Charles Marshall, was also a theatrical scene painter — a fact which might explain so embroidered and romantic a view of the town.

123. A view of Lyme Regis in the 1840s. The house on the extreme left has since fallen victim to cliff erosion. Ironically, it was the soft blue lias of the surrounding cliffs that was by then Lyme's principal export. Stone gangs worked the cliffs, first loading the limestone into barges then transferring it to the ships docked at the Cobb. If the Cobb was empty it was temporarily dumped in a corner of the bay known as the Heap.

124. The bottom of Broad Street, Lyme Regis, from Bell Cliff, in about 1843. The thin three storey house on the corner was the Fossil Depot. Facing it on the other side of the street and seen here with its balcony and supporting columns, was the Customs House — destroyed in the fire of 1844. The Walk beneath the balcony had been the central meeting place in the town since the construction of the first Customs House in 1548.

126. (Overleaf) The *Albion* balloon passing over Weymouth in August 1842. The *Albion* was the first balloon ever seen in Dorset. It began its ascent at the race course and was helped on its way by a band and a crowd of 16,000. Crimson and gold silk decked the car and its interior was lined with green damask. After a 1½ hour flight, it descended near Bere Regis, where it so bewildered the locals that many took shelter or hid.

125. The fire at Lyme Regis, May 1844. The fire started in a baker's loft used for storing furze for his ovens. It soon spread, forcing the crews of 3 naval cutters then in port to begin working the fire-engines and pulling down houses. It was a formidable task. There had been no rain for nearly 2 months and 'nothing could arrest the progress of the flames'. 40 buildings were destroyed, amongst them the Shambles, Customs House and 5 inns. According to Mary Anning, the Shambles was deliberately demolished to stop the fire spreading.

# Transport

127. A carrier's cart in the Market Place, Blandford, in the 1850s. Prior to the arrival of the railway, the pack-horse and carrier's cart were the main methods of transport. A contemporary directory lists 26 carriers for Blandford alone, some travelling as far afield as Bristol and London at an average of 7 m.p.h.

128, 129. Two views of the ferry at Smallmouth prior to the opening of the bridge linking Portland to Wyke Regis in 1839. During the Great Storm of 1824 the Ferry House was washed away and the 'poor, honest, worthy old ferryman, after 30 years service, fell a victim to his own benevolence'. He was drowned attempting to save a dragoon. The two ships in the top illustration attended the royal family during their visit to Weymouth in 1791: they were the 74 gun *Magnificent* and the frigate *Southampton*.

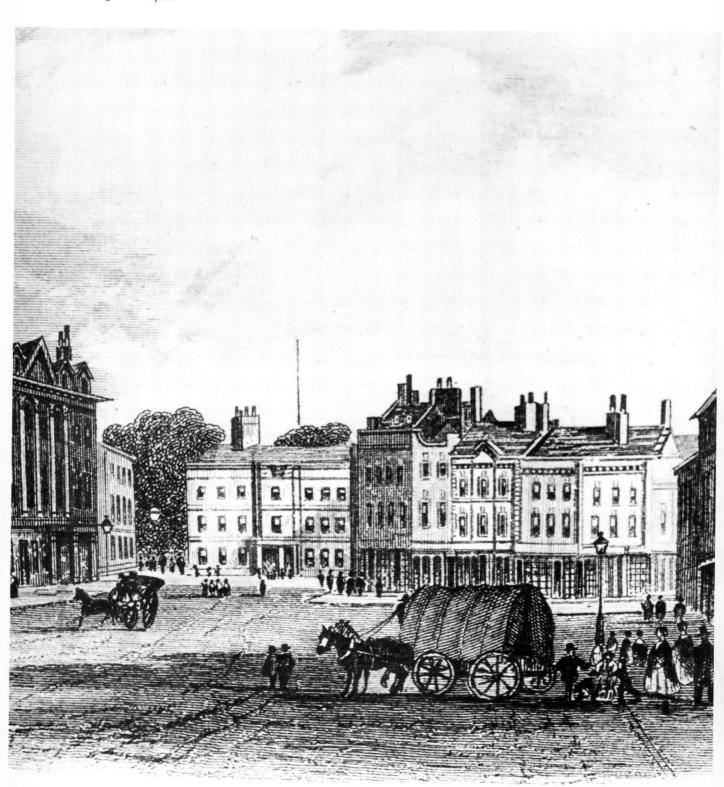

130. Woolcotts London & Exeter Warehouse, Green Hill, Sherborne; a painting by Eliza King, one of the two women with umbrellas in the foreground. The building, once the Elizabethan New Inn, was demolished in 1842. The presence of such a warehouse in Sherborne emphasizes the town's importance as a staging-post on the roads between the West Country and London.

131. Grey's Bridge and the road leading into Dorchester from the east in the 1770s: St. George's, Fordington, can be seen in the background. Grey's Bridge was built in 1747 at the expense of a Mrs. Pitt, replacing an earlier bridge on a different site. By the date of this illustration the Royal Mail provided a daily 13½ hour coach service to London.

132, 133. The arrival of the railway in Dorset in June 1847: *top,* Wimborne Station and the bridge over the Stour: *bottom,* the first train entering Dorchester South. The Southampton & Dorchester Railway was the creation of a Wimborne solicitor, Charles Castleman, and was later incorporated into the London & South Western Railway. Note the unique lay-out at Dorchester South where the two platforms, instead of facing each other, were built side by side. At its height, the Dorset railway network extended to 170 route miles of track and 59 stations and halts.

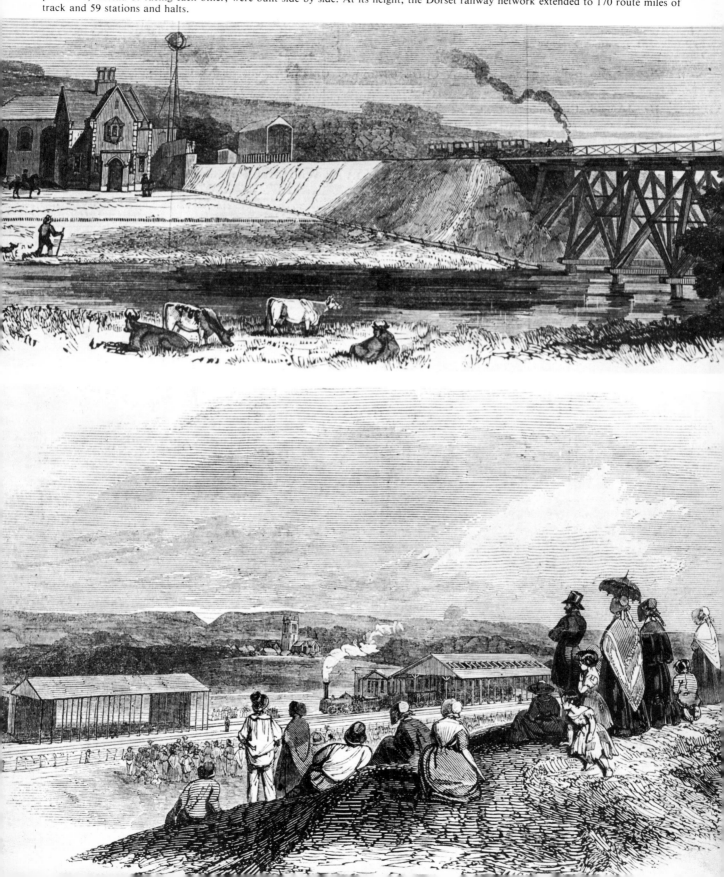

134. Bournemouth in the 1850s. Although Bournemouth did not become part of Dorset until 1974, there is a hint of prophecy about this print of the then infant resort. It is taken from a book entitled *Seventy-Two Views of Dorset*.